SCIENCE Workbook

Level 4

MOONSTONE

Published in Moonstone
by Rupa Publications India Pvt. Ltd 2022
7/16, Ansari Road, Daryaganj
New Delhi 110002

Sales centres:
Allahabad Bengaluru Chennai
Hyderabad Jaipur Kathmandu
Kolkata Mumbai

Copyright © Rupa Publications India Pvt. Ltd 2022

The views and opinions expressed in this book are
the authors' own and the facts are as reported by them
which have been verified to the extent possible,
and the publishers are not in any way liable for the same.

All rights reserved.
No part of this publication may be reproduced, transmitted,
or stored in a retrieval system, in any form or by any means,
electronic, mechanical, photocopying, recording or otherwise,
without the prior permission of the publisher.

ISBN: 978-93-5520-700-5

First impression 2022

10 9 8 7 6 5 4 3 2 1

The moral right of the authors has been asserted.

Printed in India
This book is sold subject to the condition that it shall not,
by way of trade or otherwise, be lent, resold, hired out, or otherwise
circulated, without the publisher's prior consent, in any form of binding
or cover other than that in which it is published.

Contents

Food for Plants 4

Adaptation in Plants 7

Animals and Their Babies. 10

Adaptation in Animals 13

Keeping Our Earth Green 16

Balanced Diet. 19

Digestion of Food. 22

Circulatory System 25

Clothes We Wear 28

Safety Measures 31

States of Matter 34

Force, Work and Energy. 37

The Solar System 40

Answer 46

Food for Plants

1. Fill in the blanks.

a. The _____ of a plant makes food.

b. The flat part of a leaf is called the _____.

c. Plants transport air through tiny openings called _____.

d. The food prepared by plants is called _____.

e. The leaves appear green due to the presence of _____.

2. Write T for true statements and F for false ones.

a. A leaf can have many veins.

b. The stem of a plant has no function.

c. The leaves of a banana tree are very small.

d. Plants breathe through stomata.

e. Chlorophyll makes the leaves appear red.

3. Name the part of the plant:

a. That absorbs water and minerals from the soil _____

b. That makes food for the plant _____

c. That helps to transport food and water _____

d. That helps the plant to breathe _____

e. That changes into a fruit _____

4. **Match the following.**

   Column A   **Column B**

   a. Shoot   Prepares food

   b. Flower   Makes leaves look green

   c. Leaf   Grows above the soil

   d. Roots   Changes into fruit

   e. Chlorophyll   Grows below the soil

5. **Answer the following questions.**

   a. Name the raw materials which a plant needs to make its food.
   _____

   b. Why do leaves have stomata?
   _____

   c. What is the most important function of a leaf?
   _____

   d. Name the different parts of a leaf.
   _____

   e. What is the function of flowers?
   _____

   f. How do plants use the food they prepare?
   _____

6. Think and write

There are some plants which have some leaves or none at all. Can you think and write how such plants make their food?

_____

_____

_____

_____

7. Activity time

Collect the seeds of different fruits and compare them. Draw them in your notebook and list the differences between them.

Adaptation in Plants

1. **Fill in the blanks with the correct words.**

   a. Trees that grow in hot climate shed most of their leaves in the _____ season. (spring/autumn)

   b. Teak and rubber trees are also called _____ trees. (evergreen/waxy)

   c. Cactus plant stores water in its _____. (stem/roots)

   d. Coastal plants can survive on _____ water. (sticky/salty)

   e. Leaves of _____ plants absorb gases dissolved in water. (underwater/floating)

2. **Write T for true statements and F for false ones.**

   a. The roots of mangroves grow above the ground.

   b. Plants that live in water are called coastal plants.

   c. Desert plants adapt themselves to give shade to the travellers.

   d. Plants that grow on mountains have needle like leaves.

   e. Many plants are used for medicinal purposes also.

3. **Give two examples for the following.**

   a. Mountain plants _____ _____

   b. Insectivorous plants _____ _____

   c. Desert plants _____ _____

   d. Aquatic plants _____ _____

   e. Non-green plants _____ _____

4.   Match the following.

   Column A   **Column B**

   a.   Breathing roots   Underplants

   b.   Wax coating on leaves   Swamp

   c.   Thorns in place of leaves   Floating plants

   d.   Absent of stomata   Mountain

   e.   Spongy stem   Desert

5.   Answer the following questions.

a.   Why do plants need to adapt?

   _____

b.   How do desert plants survive?

   _____

c.   What are some specific features of aquatic plants?

   _____

d.   What are insectivorous plants? Name two such plants.

   _____

e.   How do plants in hilly areas adapt to cold and snow?

   _____

6. **Think and write**

   Some plants can also be kept indoors. Can you think and write how these plants prepare their food in the absence of sunlight?

   _____

   _____

   _____

   _____

7. **Activity time**

   Select any terrestrial region. Collect pictures of various plants which grow in that region. Paste them on a chart paper and write how they adapt to live in that particular region.

Animals and Their Babies

1. **Fill in the blanks with the correct words.**

a. Animals that give birth to young ones are called _____.

b. An egg has a white jelly like substance called _____.

c. _____ lay eggs with a hard outer shell.

d. Birds, insects, reptiles and fishes lay _____.

e. Kangaroos have a _____ on their body to carry their young ones.

2. **Match the names of the animals to their young ones.**

   Column A   **Column B**
   a. Frog   Nymph
   b. Butterfly   Cub
   c. Cockroach   Tadpole
   d. Bird   Caterpillar
   e. Lion   Chick

3. **Describe the following terms.**

a. Life-span   _____

b. Life-cycle   _____

c. Hatching   _____

d. Reproduction   _____

e. Cocoon   _____

4. Read the names of the animals and place them under the correct section in the table given below.

| Frog | Tiger | Bear | Tortoise | Whale |
| Parrot | Cat | Snake | Elephant | Lizard |

Animals that lay eggs	Animals that produce babies

5. Answer the following questions.

a. What is incubation?
_____

b. Why do animals reproduce?
_____

c. What are the stages in the life-cycle of a frog?
_____

d. Name two mammals which live in water.
_____

e. Describe the life cycle of a butterfly.
_____

6. **Think and write**

   Inside the egg, the embryo grows until it hatches. What is the source of nutrients for the embryo inside the egg? Can you think and write?

   _____

   _____

   _____

   _____

   _____

7. **Activity time**

   Make a flip book showing the life-cycle of any animal. Show all the stages from an embryo to an adult. Share with your friends.

Adaptation in Animals

1. **Fill in the blanks with the correct words.**

   a. Aquatic animals breathe through their _____.

   b. _____ can live both on land and in water.

   c. Fishes have _____ to swim in water.

   d. Mammals have _____ on their body.

   e. Polar animals have a thick layer of fat under their skin called _____.

2. **Write T for true statements and F for false ones.**

   a. Aquatic animals have fins or paddles to swim. ☐

   b. Animals hibernate to escape the summer season. ☐

   c. Pandas are fastest runners among all land animals. ☐

   d. Endangered animals need protection. ☐

   e. Camouflaging is a unique characteristic of sea animals. ☐

3. **Name two animals which are:**

   a. Vertebrates _____ _____

   b. Invertebrates _____ _____

   c. Flightless birds _____ _____

d.   Hibernate   _____   _____

e.   Extinct   _____   _____

4. Give one word for the following.

a.   Animals which are in danger of getting extinct.

   _____

b.   Movement of flocks of birds from a colder to a warmer region.

   _____

c.   The animal on which another animal lives and feeds.

   _____

d.   Blending body colour with the surroundings.

   _____

e.   Land animals that live mostly on the trees.

   _____

5. Answer the following questions.

a.   Who are scavengers?

   _____

b.   What are parasites?

   _____

c. Why are some animals placed under the endangered category?

   _____

d. Which features of amphibians help them to live both on land and in water?

   _____

e. Which features of polar animals help them to survive in the cold?

   _____

6. **Think and write**

   Why are some animals in the endangered category? What can we do to protect them and help their population grow?

   _____

   _____

   _____

   _____

7. **Activity time**

   There are some birds which do not fly. Explore and find out the various conditions under which they adapted to being flightless birds.

Keeping Our Earth Green

1. **Fill in the blanks with the correct words.**

a. Trees purify _____ for us. (air/water)

b. We depend on the _____ for our basic needs. (pollution/environment)

c. Soil erosion is caused by _____ trees. (cutting/planting)

d. Vehicles should be checked regularly to _____ pollution. (control/increase)

e. Using polluted water can cause _____. (diseases/rain)

2. **Write T for true statements and F for false ones.**

a. World environment day is celebrated on 5 June every year. ☐

b. Healthy lungs are black in colour. ☐

c. Soil erosion occurs due to earthquakes. ☐

d. Waste from households and industries cause pollution. ☐

e. Recycling objects is a waste of time. ☐

3. **Name two things which:**

a. Emit smoke _____, _____

b. Pollute water _____, _____

c. Contain chemicals _____, _____

d. Purify air _____, _____

e. Can be recycled _____, _____

4. Write three ways in which we pollute:

a. Air

_____

_____

_____

b. Water

_____

_____

_____

5. Answer the following questions.

a. What is deforestation?

_____

b. What is pollution?

_____

c. What is the effect of air pollution on human beings?

_____

d. What is soil erosion?

_____

e. What is the effect of water pollution on aquatic animals?

_____

6. Think and write

We unknowingly damage the environment in our daily life. Identify some such activities and write how you can contribute to make the environment healthy.

_____

_____

_____

_____

7. Activity time

Instead of throwing away, collect old cola cans, plastic bottles and recycle them. Make useful materials with them and display in the art and craft section of your class.

Balanced Diet

1. **Fill in the blanks with the correct words.**

   a. Our body needs _____ which are present in food items.

   b. Fats keep our body _____.

   c. People who do a lot of physical work need more _____.

   d. Nearly 70% of our body weight is _____ only.

   e. _____ is called a complete food.

2. **Name the nutrient which:**

   a. Helps us to grow   _____

   b. Gives us energy to do work   _____

   c. Protects us from diseases   _____

   d. Keeps our body warm   _____

   e. Helps in making blood   _____

3. **Name two food items which contain the following nutrients.**

   a. Carbohydrates   _____   _____

   b. Roughage   _____   _____

   c. Proteins   _____   _____

   d. Fats   _____   _____

   e. Vitamins and Minerals   _____   _____

4. Rearrange the words to form correct statements.

a. drink/ plenty/ we should/ everyday/ of water

_____

b. unhealthy/ late is/ staying up/ for us

_____

c. in formation/ helps/ of blood/ iron

_____

d. body-building/ are called/ foods/ proteins

_____

e. contain/ vitamins and/ fruits and/ minerals/ vegetables

_____

5. Answer the following questions.

a. What are nutrients?

_____

b. Which parts of our body need calcium?

_____

c. What is a balanced diet?

_____

d. Why is roughage useful for us?

_____

e. Why do we need to preserve food?

_____

6. Think and write

Molly eats a balanced diet but she still feels tired every evening. The doctor told her to exercise daily and to sleep on time. Can you explain how exercise and sleeping on time will help her?

_____

_____

_____

_____

7. Activity time

There are different ways to preserve food from getting spoilt. Observe and list the activities used by your parents to preserve food at your house.

Digestion of Food

1. **Fill in the blanks given below.**

a. The process of digestion starts in the _____. (stomach/mouth)

b. _____ connects the mouth to the stomach. (Tubes/Oesophagus)

c. We should _____ the food properly. (chew/throw)

d. Some _____ help in digestion of food. (bones/microbes)

e. We should not _____ immediately after eating food. (exercise/study)

2. **Match the names of the body parts to their details.**

Column A	Column B
a. Stomach	Produce digestive juices
b. Mouth	Absorb water from the Indigestible food matter
c. Liver	Breaking of food into pieces
d. Small intestine	A sac-like organ
e. Large intestine	Absorbs all the nutrients from food

3. **Name two diseases that are caused by:**

a. Bacteria _____   _____

b. Protozoa _____   _____

c. Virus _____   _____

d. Fungi _____   _____

4. Rearrange the words to form correct statements.

a. before and after/ wash your/ every meal/ hands

_____

b. food/ fresh and/ always eat/ well-cooked

_____

c. useful/ or harmful/ can be/ to humans/ microbes

_____

d. your mouth/ after meals/ properly/ rinse

_____

e. only be seen/ microscope/ microbes can/ using a

_____

5. Answer the following questions.

a. What is digestion?

_____

b. Name the organs which help in digestion of food.

_____

c. What is the role of liver in digestion of food?

_____

d. What are microbes?

_____

e. Name four types of microbes.

_____

6. **Think and write**

As soon as we start chewing, a liquid is secreted by the glands in our mouth. Can you tell the name and function of this liquid?

_____

_____

_____

_____

7. **Activity time**

Some microbes are used to make food items like bread and curd. Find out the names of the microbes and the food items which can be prepared using them.

Circulatory System

1. **Fill in the blanks with the correct words.**

   a. Circulatory system performs _____ in our body. (excretion/transportation)

   b. Heart pumps _____ to all the body parts. (blood/air)

   c. _____ run through the entire body. (Heart/Blood vessels)

   d. Blood contains oxygen, water and _____. (food/nutrients)

   e. _____, veins and capillaries are the three types of blood vessels. (Arteries/Tubes)

2. **Write T for true statements and F for false ones.**

   a. Stomach is an important organ of our circulatory system.

   b. All the blood vessels are thin tubes.

   c. The lungs pump the blood to all the parts of our body.

   d. Heart has three bones to keep it in place.

   e. Our hair contains the maximum number of blood vessels.

3. **Answer the following questions.**

   a. What is the main function of the circulatory system?
   _____

   b. Name the organs of the circulatory system.
   _____

c. Name the three types of blood vessels.

   _____

d. What is the function of blood in our body?

   _____

e. Define the structure of heart.

   _____

4. Match the names of the body parts to their details.

Column A	Column B
a. Heart	Transported by blood
b. Blood	Pumps the blood
c. Veins	Thin tubes connected to veins and arteries
d. Oxygen	Transport oxygen rich blood
e. Capillaries	Fluid containing minerals

5. Draw and label the structure of heart in the space below.

6. Think and write

Our heart beats and facilitates the flow of blood in our body. Think about the different activities which make your heart beat faster and explain what you feel at those moments.

_____

_____

_____

_____

7. Activity time

Use wool of different colours to make a model of circulatory system in your activity file. Explore how the oxygen from our lungs is mixed into the blood.

Clothes We Wear

1. **Fill in the blanks with the correct words.**

a. Cotton clothes protect us from the heat of the _____. (rain/sun)

b. _____ was the first synthetic fibre produced by humans. (Rayon/Nylon)

c. Each yarn is made up of many thin strands called _____. (fibre/thread)

d. Animal hair which is used for making clothes is called _____. (wig/fur)

e. All the clothes should be washed with _____. (detergent/bleach)

2. **Write T for true statements and F for false ones.**

a. Woollen clothes are waterproof to keep us warm.

b. Fabrics are made by weaving or knitting the yarns together.

c. Uniforms are used to resemble the seasons.

d. Clothes should not be washed with detergent.

e. Nylon and polyester are synthetic fibres.

3. **Match these traditional clothes with the name of their originating country.**

Column A	Column B
a. Kimono	Indonesia
b. Poncho	Nigeria
c. Batik	Japan
d. Gele	France
e. Beret	Chile

4. Write Natural or Synthetic to categorize the following fibres.

a. Cotton _____

b. Acrylic _____

c. Wool _____

d. Jute _____

e. Rayon _____

f. Hemp _____

g. Polyester _____

h. Cashmere _____

5. Answer the following questions.

a. Name the two types of fibres.

_____

b. How should silk and woollen clothes be stored?

_____

c. How are natural fibres different from synthetic fibres?

_____

d. Name three things which should be used to take care of clothes.

_____

e. What are raincoats and umbrellas made of?

   _____

6. **Think and write**

   Collect the samples of synthetic and natural fibres and compare them. Examine and write which fibres are stronger and durable. Can you also explain why?

   _____

   _____

   _____

   _____

   _____

7. **Activity time**

   Make a story of a fibre showing how it makes friends with other fibres and was weaved into bonds to make a perfect piece of cloth. Give a title to your story.

Safety Measures

1. **Fill in the blanks using the correct word.**

   a. We should not play in the _____. (kitchen/room)

   b. Leaving toys lying on the floor is _____. (dangerous/safe)

   c. Always swim in the presence of an _____. (animal/adult)

   d. Climbing on the _____ can injure us. (bed/desk)

   e. Use tongs to handle _____ objects. (hot/round)

2. **Write T for true statements and F for false ones.**

   a. We should always remember our address and phone number.

   b. We should eat the things given by strangers.

   c. Climbing fence is dangerous.

   d. We should shout for help when in danger.

   e. Teasing animals is dangerous.

3. **Rewrite the sentences using the antonyms of the underlined words to correct them.**

   a. <u>Never</u> keep a first-aid box at home.

   _____

   b. We should touch the electric switches with <u>wet</u> hands.

   _____

c. Synthetic clothes <u>cannot</u> catch fire.

_____

d. We should walk on the <u>right</u> side of the road.

_____

e. <u>Disobey</u> the traffic signals on the road.

_____

4. **Draw and colour four road signs observed by you on the road. Also write down what they symbolize in the given space.**

1.	2.
3.	4.

5. **Answer the following questions.**

a. What is first-aid?
_____

b. Why is first-aid important?
_____

c. What should you do in case of a fire in your school?
_____

d. Who can provide first-aid?
_____

e. Why should we follow safety rules?
_____

6. **Think and write**

Your friend has been bitten by an insect on the hand. His hand is looking red, swollen and is burning. Explain how will you help your friend?

_____

_____

_____

7. **Activity time**

Make a list of things you need for making a first-aid box. Use an old shoe box and make your own first-aid box containing at least five useful things.

Test Yourself 1

1. Read the statements and answer in one word.

a. Yellow sticky layer that covers unhealthy teeth. _____

b. The process of shedding old skin. _____

c. An animal which can camouflage. _____

d. The name given to young cockroach. _____

e. The teeth which help in tearing of food. _____

f. An organ which secretes digestive juices. _____

g. The method to extract marbles from water. _____

h. A simple machine used for cutting paper and cloth. _____

2. Complete the sentences given below.

a. Raincoats do not absorb water because

_____

b. The streamlined body of a fish helps it to

_____

c. Friction is the force which

_____

d. In the dry cleaning process, clothes are

_____

e. Eating too many sweets can _____

f. Leaves are also called the _____

3. **Name the energy used to:**

a. Cook food _____

b. Run a car _____

c. Sail a boat _____

d. Light a bulb _____

e. Move the windmill _____

f. Make food by plants _____

g. Iron the clothes _____

h. Nail a screw in wall _____

4. **Match the following.**

Column A   Column B

a. Chlorophyll   Simple machine

b. Pulley   Rich in nutrients

c. Hinge joint   Plants

d. Loamy soil   Circulatory system

e. Heart   Hydro energy

f. Water   Elbow joint

35

States of Matter

1. **Fill in the blanks with the correct words.**

   a. All matter is made up of small _____. (drops/particles)

   b. A solute and solvent together form a _____. (particle/solution)

   c. Sugar and salt are examples of _____. (solute/solvent)

   d. Rocks are _____ in water. (soluble/insoluble)

   e. _____ can flow easily. (Solids/Liquids)

2. **Answer in one word.**

   a. Process by which a solid can be converted into liquid. _____

   b. Process by which a solid changes into gas directly. _____

   c. Process by which liquid changes into a solid. _____

   d. Process by which gas changes into liquid. _____

   e. Method by which insoluble particles can be extracted from a solution. _____

3. **Define the following terms:**

   a. Matter _____

   b. Solvent _____

   c. Solute _____

d. Solution _____

4. **Answer the following questions.**

a. How are solids different from gases?
   _____

b. What is the difference between melting and freezing?
   _____

c. What are soluble substances? Give two examples.
   _____

d. What are insoluble substances? Give two examples.
   _____

e. How can you distinguish between soluble and insoluble substances?
   _____

5. **Complete the table given below.**

State of matter	Space between particles	Shape	Feel when touched	Two examples
Solid				
Liquid				
Gas				

6. **Think and write**

You have dissolved a lot of salt in a glass of water by mistake. Think and write a possible way through which you can get the salt back in solid form.

_____

_____

_____

_____

7. **Activity time**

Sieving, filtration and hand picking methods are used in daily life to separate the particles of a mixture. Look for some activities in your daily life where you need to separate things.

Force, Work and Energy

1. **Fill in the blanks with the correct words.**

a. Friction _____ the motion of an object. (resists/starts)

b. Simple machines make our work _____. (tough/easy)

c. There is _____ friction on a smooth surface. (more/less)

d. Plants use _____ energy to make their food. (solar/hydro)

e. _____ are built to collect and use hydro power. (Dams/Windmills)

2. **Write T for true statements and F for false ones.**

a. Gravity and friction are the same forces. ☐

b. Nothing can move in the absence of frictional force. ☐

c. A wheel is a simple machine. ☐

d. Energy can change from one form to another. ☐

e. Throwing a ball does not need force. ☐

3. **Write two examples for each of the following.**

a. Lever _____, _____

b. Gravity _____, _____

c. Wedge _____, _____

d. Friction _____, _____

e. Screw _____, _____

4. Replace the underlined words and rewrite the correct sentences.

a. Energy received from the water is called <u>solar</u> energy.

_____

b. We use a pulley to draw <u>sand</u> from a well.

_____

c. A <u>complex</u> machine makes our work easier and faster.

_____

d. The energy of moving water is called <u>smart</u> energy.

_____

e. Gravitational force pulls objects <u>upwards</u>.

_____

5. Answer the following questions.

a. What is force?

_____

b. What is work?

_____

c. Why do we need energy?

   _____

d. What is frictional force?

   _____

e. How do simple machines help us?

   _____

6. **Think and write**

   A lot of countries have started to use solar energy in place of fossil fuels. Think and explain how it is useful for both people and environment.

   _____

   _____

   _____

7. **Activity time**

   We use many simple machines in our daily life. Make a list of simple machines you use at your home. Is there any tool which has two simple machines in it? If yes, name it.

The Solar System

1. **Fill in the blanks with the correct words.**

   a. _____ is the fifth planet from the sun.

   b. Saturn is the only planet with _____.

   c. _____ are the glowing balls of gases.

   d. The name of our galaxy is _____.

   e. The innermost core of the Earth is made up of _____.

2. **Write T for true statements and F for false ones.**

   a. Moon has an atmosphere just like the Earth's. ☐

   b. Equator and axis are imaginary lines. ☐

   c. The Earth completes one revolution in 24 hours. ☐

   d. Pluto is called a dwarf planet. ☐

   e. Moon is the only natural satellite of the Earth. ☐

3. **Answer in one word.**

   a. A constellation _____

   b. A natural satellite _____

   c. A man-made satellite _____

   d. The red planet _____

   e. A dwarf planet _____

4. **Define the terms:**

a. Solar system _____

_____

b. Satellite _____

_____

c. Moon _____

_____

d. Stars _____

_____

e. Equator _____

_____

5. **Answer the following questions.**

a. What are dwarf planets?

_____

b. At what angle is the axis of the Earth tilted?

_____

c. What causes day and night? Explain briefly.

_____

d. What provides us light during the night?

_____

e. What is the need of equator?

_____

6. **Think and write**

   Imagine what would happen if one day, the Earth stops rotating. Describe the situation in your own words.

   _____

   _____

   _____

   _____

   _____

7. **Activity time**

   Colour a plastic ball to make a model of the Earth. Show the imaginary lines i.e. axis and equator on your model.

Test Yourself 2

1. Read the statements and answer in one word.

a. Trees which don't lose their leaves through the year. _____

b. Doctor who is a tooth specialist. _____

c. Function of the large intestine in the digestion process. _____

d. The two imaginary lines we draw on a globe. _____

e. A force which pulls everything towards the ground. _____

f. An organ that connects mouth to stomach. _____

g. A white jelly like substance in egg. _____

h. The first synthetic fibre made by humans. _____

2. Match the following.

Column A	Column B
a. Mangroves	Coastal area
b. Pondweed	Floating plant
c. Pitcher plant	Swamps
d. Indian pipe	Desert
e. Barrel	Evergreen tree
f. Coconut	Insectivorous plant
g. Rubber tree	Non-green plant
h. Water hyacinth	Underwater plant

3. Give two examples for each of the following.

a. Lever _____ _____

b. Dwarf planets _____ _____

c. Inclined plane _____ _____

d. Wheel and axle _____ _____

e. Constellations _____ _____

f. Microbes _____ _____

g. Forces _____ _____

h. Forms of energy _____ _____

4. Make the correct words from the jumbled letters and write the answer.

a. Trees hold it to prevent erosion. I L S O _____

b. Uppermost layer of soil. S I T O L O P _____

c. The butterfly grows in it. A P P U _____

d. It is a simple machine. E W S R C _____

e. Plants release it into air. Y E G O X N _____

f. Moving air. N D I W _____

g. Hottest planet of solar system. U S V E N _____

h. Planets revolve on this path. R O B T I _____

Answers

Food for Plants

1. a. leaves b. lamina
   c. stomata d. starch
   e. chlorophyll
2. a. T b. F c. F d. T e. F
3. a. Root b. Leaves
   c. Stem d. Stomata
   e. Flower
4. a. Grows above the soil
   b. Changes into fruit
   c. Prepares food
   d. Grow below the soil
   e. Makes leaves look green

Adaptation in Plants

1. a. autumn b. evergreen
   c. stem d. salty
   e. underwater
2. a. T b. F c. F d. T e. T
3. a. Pine, Bamboo
   b. Venus flytrap, Pitcher plant
   c. Cactus, Barrel, Pine
   d. Water Hyacinth, Duck weed
   e. Mushroom, Yeast
4. a. Swamp b. Mountain
   c. Desert d. Underwater plants
   e. Floating plants

Animals and Their Babies

1. a. mammals b. albumen
   c. Birds d. eggs
   e. pouch
2. a. Tadpole b. Caterpillar
   c. Nymph d. Chick
   e. Cub
3. a. The time period for which a living being is alive is its life span.
   b. Stages of development of a living being from birth to death.
   c. Breaking of an egg by young ones of animals to come outside.
   d. The ability of living beings to produce more beings of similar kind.
   e. Cocoon is the case spun by the larvae of insects to protect the pupa.
4. Animals that lay eggs: frog, tortoise, snake, lizard, parrot
   Animals that produce babies: tiger, bear, whale, cat, elephant

Adaptation in Animals

1. a. gills b. Amphibians
   c. fins d. hair
   e. blubber
2. a. T b. F c. F d. T e. F
3. a. Fish, Horse
   b. Ant, Earthworm
   c. Kiwi, Ostrich
   d. Frog, Lizard, Snake
   e. Dodo, Monk seal, Sea cow
4. a. Endangered animals b. Migration
   c. Host d. Camouflaging
   e. Arboreal

Keeping Our Earth Green

1. a. air b. environment
   c. cutting d. control
   e. diseases
2. a. T b. F c. F d. T e. F
3. a. Car, Factories
   b. Sewage, Oil spills in ocean
   c. Pesticides, Oil, Insecticides
   d. Trees, Plants
   e. Newspaper, Tin cans
4. a. Using automobiles, Burning wastes, Cutting trees
   b. Household sewage, Industry waste, Plastic waste thrown in rivers

Balanced Diet

1. a. nutrients
   b. warm
   c. carbohydrates
   d. water
   e. Milk
2. a. Proteins
   b. Carbohydrates
   c. Vitamins and Minerals
   d. Fats
   e. Iron
3. a. Potato, Cereals
   b. Fruits, Salad
   c. Cheese, Pulses
   d. Coconut oil, Nuts
   e. Fruits, Vegetables
4. a. We should drink plenty of water every day.
   b. Staying up late is unhealthy for us.
   c. Iron helps in the formation of blood.
   d. Proteins are called body-building food.
   e. Fruits and vegetables contain vitamins and minerals.

Digestion of Food

1. a. mouth b. Oesophagus
   c. chew d. microbes
   e. exercise
2. a. A sac-like organ
   b. Breaking of food into pieces
   c. Produce digestive juices
   d. Absorbs all the nutrients from food
   e. Absorb water from the indigestible food matter
3. a. Tuberculosis, Tetanus
   b. Malaria, Dysentery
   c. Common cold, Polio
   d. Athlete's foot, Meningitis
4. a. Wash your hands before and after every meal.
   b. Always eat fresh and well-cooked food.
   c. Microbes can be useful or harmful to humans.
   d. Rinse your mouth properly after meals.
   e. Microbes can only be seen using a microscope.

Circulatory System

1. a. transportation
   b. blood c. Blood vessels
   d. nutrients e. Arteries
2. a. F b. T c. F d. F e. F
4. a. Pumps the blood
   b. Fluid containing minerals
   c. Transport oxygen rich blood
   d. Transported by blood
   e. Thin tubes connected to veins and arteries

Clothes We Wear

1. a. sun b. Nylon
   c. fibre d. fur
   e. detergent
2. a. F b. T c. F d. F e. T
3. a. Japan b. Chile
   c. Indonesia d. Nigeria
   e. France
4. a. Natural b. Synthetic
   c. Natural d. Natural
   e. Synthetic f. Natural
   g. Synthetic h. Natural

Safety Measures

1. a. kitchen b. dangerous
   c. adult d. desk
   e. hot
2. a. T b. F c. T d. T e. T
3. a. Always b. dry c. can
   d. left e. Obey

Test Yourself 1

1. a. Plaque b. Moulting
   c. Chameleon d. Nymph
   e. Incisors f. Liver
   g. Filtration h. Scissor
2. a. Raincoats are made from waterproof material.
   b. Swim across the water easily.
   c. Slows down the speed of moving object.
   d. Cleaned without using water.
   e. Damage our teeth.
   f. Food factory of plants.
3. a. Heat energy
   b. Electrical energy, Mechanical energy
   c. Hydro energy, Wind energy
   d. Electrical energy
   e. Wind energy
   f. Solar energy, Chemical energy
   g. Heat energy, Electrical energy
   h. Mechanical energy
4. a. Plants b. Simple machine
   c. Elbow joint d. Rich in nutrients
   e. Circulatory system f. Hydro energy

States of Matter

1. a. particles b. solution
   c. solute d. insoluble
   e. Liquids
2. a. Melting b. Sublimation
   c. Freezing d. Condensation
   e. Filtration

Force, Work and Energy

1. a. resists b. easy
   c. less d. solar
   e. Dams
2. a. F b. F c. T d. T e. F
4. a. hydro b. water
   c. simple d. kinetic
   e. downwards

Solar System

1. a. Jupiter b. rings
   c. Stars d. Milky Way
   e. Iron-Nickel alloy
2. a. F b. T c. F d. T e. T
3. a. Orion b. Moon c. Sputnik 1
   d. Mars e. Pluto, Ceres

Test Yourself 2

1. a. Evergreen b. Dentist
   c. Absorbing water d. Latitudes and Longitudes
   e. Gravity f. Oesophagus
   g. Albumen h. Nylon
2. a. Swamps b. Underwater plant
   c. Insectivorous plant d. Non-green plant
   e. Desert f. Coastal area
   g. Evergreen tree h. Floating plant
4. a. Soil b. Topsoil c. Pupa
   d. Screw e. Oxygen f. Wind
   g. Venus h. Orbit

www.ingramcontent.com/pod-product-compliance
Lightning Source LLC
Chambersburg PA
CBHW040057160426

43192CB00002B/91